- THE -
YORKSHIRE
MOORS & COAST

John Potter

MYRIAD

Staithes has a dramatic setting on the rugged stretch of coast north of Whitby, tucked into a cleft of rock which forms a natural harbour. Staithes' white-painted cottages are haphazardly perched on any available space.

Right: just above Runswick Bay's long sandy beach the boat park with its many cobles (small wooden fishing boats) is a honeypot for artists and photographers.

Left: Sandsend is a pretty little fishing village located at the foot of steep Lythe Bank where the sandy beach that begins at Whitby, just two miles to the south, comes to an abrupt end at the foot of the cliffs at Sandsend Ness (below). Sandsend has some of the best surf on this stretch of coastline and has a reputation as a local surfer's paradise. The village has picturesque stone cottages set against a backdrop of cliffs.

Often referred to as Captain Cook's Country, the seaside town of Whitby and the surrounding countryside, from where the young James Cook drew inspiration and learned the seafarer's trade, is steeped in maritime history. Cook was born in Marton, a small village just south of Middlesbrough. His first job was in Staithes, where he assisted the merchant William Sanderson. In 1746 he took up residence in John Walker's house, an elegant 17th-century harbourside house in Grape Lane, where he served his apprenticeship and learned about navigation and seamanship. The house is now the Captain Cook Memorial Museum.

The steep cliffs at Saltwick Bay, one mile south-east of Whitby, are constantly being eroded by wind and sea. The shelving beach here is littered with the wreckage of boats which have foundered on this dangerous stretch of coast.

The picturesque fishing village of Robin Hood's Bay, viewed below from the clifftop path, is one of the highlights of any visit to the Yorkshire coast. Its steep winding streets and cobbled ginnels (narrow alleyways between houses) made the village an ideal spot for smuggling – one of the area's main industries in the past.

Perched on a rocky headland above the harbour, the ruined Norman castle dominates Scarborough's skyline. On the other side of the bay, beneath the South Cliff promenade, lies the town's Spa Complex with its superb parks, gardens, theatres and conference hall. The majestic Grand Hotel, completed in 1867, when Scarborough became established as Britain's first seaside resort, overlooks the South Beach.

At 400ft (122m), Bempton has some of the highest cliffs on the east coast of Britain, and is famous as a seabird nature reserve, featuring the only gannet colony in mainland Britain. The cliffs stretch for approximately six miles from Flamborough Head north towards Filey. The historic village of Bempton, four miles north of Bridlington, is the ideal starting point for a clifftop walk.

The coastline at Flamborough is magnificent: Thornwick Bay (below) is just one of the many sheltered shingle coves fronting the sea where the adjacent cliffs have sea caves and dramatic stacks.

Left: with its two glorious long sandy beaches, miles of elegant promenades and a pretty and bustling harbour, Bridlington has all the essential ingredients for a perfect family holiday.

Below: the Lighthouse Museum at Withernsea.

Right: Spurn Point, situated on the north bank of the entrance to the river Humber, is a unique habitat.

Left: the Humber Bridge was designed and built to link the communities of north Lincolnshire and Humberside.

Right: the Hull Marina occupies the site of the former Humber and Railway Docks.

Below: the gleaming glass and aluminium marine life centre called The Deep stands at the confluence of the rivers Hull and Humber.

Left: with its heather-clad moorland, fertile dales and characterful villages and market towns, the North York Moors has one of Yorkshire's most beautiful and captivating landscapes. Most of the region became a National Park in 1952.

Right: Danby Dale. This quaintly-named corner of North Yorkshire consists of two secluded valleys, Great and Little Fryup, made up of a scattering of farms and cottages. Winding off the Esk Valley the area is totally unspoilt and surrounded by magnificent purple heather-clad moors with trails and walks across the moorland. Fryup Dale is an ideal place from which to explore *Heartbeat* country, either on foot or by bike. The picturesque fishing village of Runswick Bay is just 10 miles away and the Esk Valley railway line links with the North York Moors Steam Railway at Grosmont.

Nestling in the Esk Valley, the village of Glaisdale is a past winner of the "Village of the Year" award for the North of England. The valley around Glaisdale is truly a majestic sight when viewed in winter from high up on the fellside. This photograph (below) was taken from the roadside near Low Gill Beck Farm, looking towards Glaisdale Moor.

Above: the high moorland here is dotted with grouse butts which are used to give cover for gamekeepers and shooters during the grouse season.

Right: situated in the upper Esk Valley, the linear village of Castleton sits proudly on a high ridge, where the secluded valleys of Westerdale and Danby Dale come together.

Above: young Ralph Cross stands at the junction of two roads near Rosedale Head. It is said that the present cross was erected in memory of a traveller who died from exhaustion. A Danby farmer called Ralph discovered him and erected a cross where he found the body.

Above and right: Mallyan Spout, the highest waterfall on the North York Moors, near Goathland, cascades 60ft down the side of West Beck Gorge. The waterfall is close to the Mallyan Spout Hotel, opposite St Mary's church at the western edge of the village.

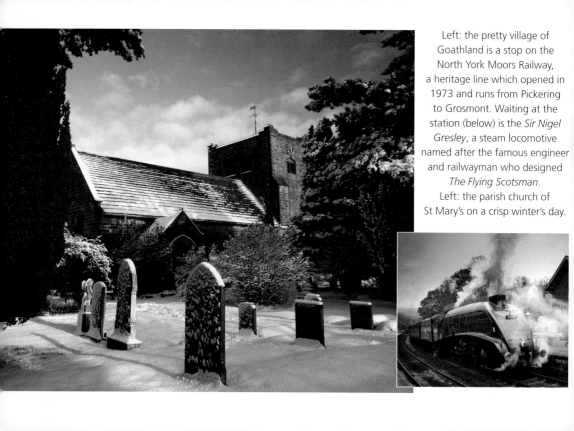

Left: the pretty village of Goathland is a stop on the North York Moors Railway, a heritage line which opened in 1973 and runs from Pickering to Grosmont. Waiting at the station (below) is the *Sir Nigel Gresley*, a steam locomotive named after the famous engineer and railwayman who designed *The Flying Scotsman*.
Left: the parish church of St Mary's on a crisp winter's day.

Rosedale is a long extended valley located in the heart of the North York Moors. It stretches out in a south-easterly direction from Westerdale Moor and Danby High Moor towards Hartoft End and Cropton Forest. The river Seven flows throughout its length gathering water from the numerous moorland springs and streams.

Below: the pretty village of Hutton-le-Hole has a broad village green where moorland sheep roam freely. The Ryedale Folk Museum depicts the life of North Yorkshire people through the centuries. Right: running between Farndale and Bilsdale, remote Bransdale consists of a few scattered farmsteads and cottages set in glorious scenery.

Left: Helmsley Castle is a spectacular ruin which once guarded the Rye valley. The early 13th-century castle is surrounded by a formidable double ditch cut from solid rock. Helmsley is one of the most attractive market towns in North Yorkshire and an ideal centre for touring the local area. A pretty stream runs through the town at the back of the market square with an elegant stone arch bridge.

Right: Rievaulx Abbey, like all Cistercian monasteries, was deliberately secluded from the outside world and this particular site in the depths of the narrow river Rye valley must have provided the monks and lay brethren with a haven of peace and solitude. The 13th-century church is reputed to have been one of the finest monastic churches in northern Britain and remains substantially intact. The site is now run by English Heritage.

Left: Whitestone Cliff on the Cleveland Way footpath looking north towards the village of Boltby. The Cleveland Way starts in the market town of Helmsley and traverses the upland ridge on the edge of the North York Moors before reaching the coast at Saltburn by Sea.

Right: just beyond Roulston Scar lies the well-known landmark, the White Horse of Kilburn, built by local teacher John Hodgson and his pupils in 1857. The White Horse, which is visible throughout large parts of the Vale of York, was intended to resemble the hill figures which are cut into the chalk downs in many parts of southern England. The best view of the horse is reported to be from two elevated benches just inside the northern boundary of Kilburn village.

Above: the pretty village of Gillamoor lies 2.5 miles (4km) north of Kirkbymoorside. The village is famously known for its Surprise View (right) at the eastern end of the hamlet, beside St Aidan's church. The view of lower Farndale from this point (right) is captivating and memorable whatever the season.

Below: the market town of Kirkbymoorside is considered by many to be the gateway to the North York Moors. All Saints church is set back from the main street; it is photographed here from a recently landscaped area on the edge of the town.

Farndale: best known for its wild daffodils in spring, Farndale attracts up to 40,000 visitors each April. The daffodil walk follows the valley bottom beside the river Dove, from Low Mill to Church Houses and the welcoming Feversham Arms.

The Hole of Horcum is a huge natural amphitheatre hollowed out of the heather-clad moor situated beside the Pickering to Whitby road. Legend has it that "The Devil's Punchbowl", as it is known locally, was made by a giant named Wade who scooped out the rocks and earth, tossing them two miles east to Blakey Topping.

Above: the village of Lastingham is now a peaceful haven but the historic Crypt Church of St Mary was once a major centre of pilgrimage. Visitors came to visit the shrine to St Chad and St Cedd who founded a monastery on this site around 645.

Above: the busy and elegant market town of Pickering is located on the southern edge of the North York Moors. It was originally a Celtic town dating from the 3rd century BC, and has a motte-and-bailey castle with Norman remnants (right). In the centre of the town is Beck Isle Museum of Rural Life.

The picturesque village of Levisham nestles above the quiet and winding wooded valley of Newton Dale, seven miles north of Pickering. The small church of St John the Baptist lies at the top of the village where the road and a footpath, which meanders across woods and fields, leads to the railway station – a stop on the North Yorks Railway – in the bottom of the valley. The station has been used as the location for a range of television programmes including *All Creatures Great and Small*, *Poirot*, *Sherlock Holmes* and *Brideshead Revisited*.

Thornton Le Dale lies just east of Pickering. This pretty village has a small green with a market cross and stocks together with gift shops, tea rooms, and a sparkling stream.

St Peter's church in Hackness houses a priceless Anglo-Saxon cross, one of the finest examples of Anglo-Saxon sculpture. The village is ideally suited for touring since it lies only five miles from the heritage coast and the seaside resorts of Whitby and Sandsend.

Westerdale, Bilsdale and Blakey Ridge offer some of the finest high moorland walks in northern England. The famous coast-to-coast trail from St Bees in Cumbria to Robin Hood's Bay crosses Blakey Ridge and another long-distance path, the 41-mile Lyke Wake Walk, is close by. All of these moorlands are dotted with large stone markers and crosses, many dating back to the Bronze Age.